BLIZZARD!

The 1888 Whiteout

by Jacqueline A. Ball

Consultant: Daniel H. Franck, Ph.D.

BEARPORT
PUBLISHING COMPANY, INC.

New York, New York

Credits

Cover, David Pollack / CORBIS; Bettmann / CORBIS; CORBIS.
Title page, Bettmann / CORBIS; 4-5, Bettmann / CORBIS; 6, Louis Pappas and Steve Stankiewitz;
6-7, AP Photo / The Herald Bulletin; 8, Bettmann / CORBIS; 8-9, AP Photo / Mark Lennihan;
10-11, The Granger Collection, New York; 12, Library of Congress Prints & Photographs Collection;
14-15, Nebraska State Historical Society Photograph Collections; 16-17, © Hulton-Deutsch
Collection/ CORBIS; 18, Bettmann / CORBIS; 19, AP Photo; 20, CORBIS; 21, The Granger Collection,
New York; 22, AP Photo/NYC Transit Authority; 23, AP Photo/Mark Lennihan; 24, 25, Bettmann /
CORBIS; 26-27, AP Photo/Ric Feld; 29, CORBIS.

Design and production by Dawn Beard Creative, Triesta Hall of Blu-Design,
and Octavo Design and Production, Inc.

Library of Congress Cataloging-in-Publication Data

Ball, Jacqueline A.
  Blizzard! : the 1888 whiteout / by Jacqueline A. Ball ; consultant, Daniel H. Franck.
      p. cm. — (X-treme disasters that changed America)
  Includes bibliographical references and index.
  ISBN 1-59716-006-7 (lib. bdg.)—ISBN 1-59716-029-6 (pbk.)
  1. Blizzards—Juvenile literature. 2. Blizzards—New York (N.Y.)—History—19th century—
Juvenile literature. 3. New York (N.Y.)—History—1865-1898—Juvenile literature. I. Title. II. Series.

  QC926.37.B35 2005
  363.34'925—dc22

                              2004020740

For more information, write to Bearport Publishing Company, Inc., 101 Fifth Avenue, Suite 6R,
New York, New York 10003. Printed in the United States of America.

1 2 3 4 5 6 7 8 9 10

Table of Contents

"We're Having a Blizzard!"

It was Sunday, March 11, 1888. In New York City, the first spring flowers were popping up. The weather was warm but rainy.

A girl named Meta (MAY–ta) was bored because she couldn't play outside. She went to bed early. Before morning, Meta woke up. A bright light filled her room.

Meta didn't look out the window. She decided to go back to sleep. Hours later she finally pulled up the window shade.

Mountains of snow covered the city. Fresh snow was still falling. The wind piled it up and blew it around.

"Mother! Father!" Meta cried. "We're having a **blizzard**!"

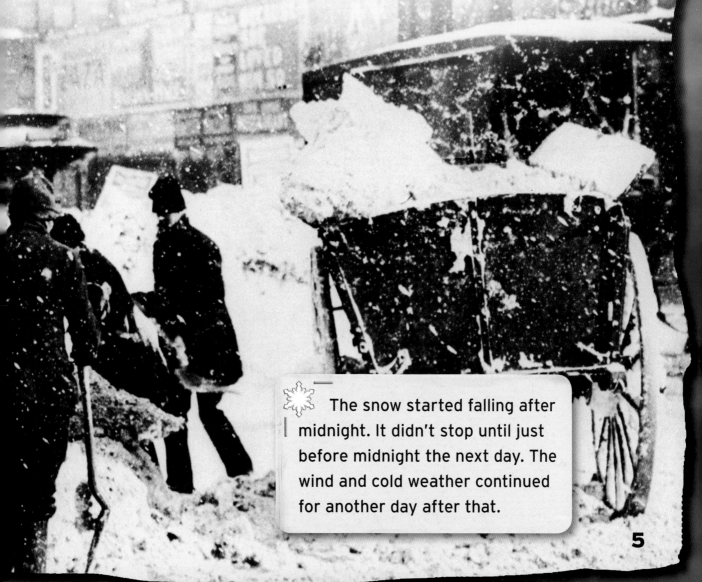

The snow started falling after midnight. It didn't stop until just before midnight the next day. The wind and cold weather continued for another day after that.

What Is a Blizzard?

Meta had heard about blizzards. They were much more forceful than regular **snowstorms**.

Scientists today say a blizzard has certain **features**. It must have winds of at least 35 miles per hour. The snow has to blow so hard that you can't see more than 500 feet in front of you. The temperature should be under 20°F. If these **conditions** last at least three hours, then it's a blizzard.

A Blizzard Forms

very cold, dry air

warm, moist air

For a blizzard to form, very cold, dry air must bump into warm, moist air.

The storm Meta watched had all these features. It would become the most famous blizzard in American history—the Blizzard of 1888.

▲ This blizzard hit Indiana on January 26, 1978. During the whiteout, more than 15 inches of snow fell. Snowdrifts were up to eight feet high.

In a blizzard, snowfall can be so heavy that it's hard to see the earth and sky. This condition is called a "whiteout."

A Chilling Wind

The blizzard lasted two days. The temperature dropped to 0°F. The winds blew at **hurricane** speeds. The storm was nicknamed *The White Hurricane.*

▲ People on the street after the Blizzard of 1888 hit New York City

▶ These New Yorkers got caught outside during a blizzard on January 8, 1996, in Brooklyn, New York.

Strong winds and cold weather are a deadly mix. Wind makes our bodies lose heat. We feel colder on a windy day than on a calm one, even if the temperature is the same. This **effect** is called the wind chill factor.

At 0°F, with winds of 48 miles per hour, uncovered flesh freezes in less than one minute. It's not safe to be outside. Since there was no warning, many people were caught in the storm.

Blizzards don't have to bring falling snow. A storm with high winds, very cold temperatures, and blowing snow can also be called a blizzard.

"Colder, but Generally Fair"

Over a hundred years ago, all the weather
forecasts were made by scientists in Washington, D.C.
There was no weather channel. There was no TV at
all. Even radio had not yet been invented. Weather
reports were sent around the country by telephone
and **telegraph**. Then local newspapers printed them.

The weather forecasters didn't work on Sundays. The last forecast before the blizzard was sent out on Saturday night. Meta's parents read about the weather in the Sunday *New York Herald*. The paper said, "Tomorrow: colder, but generally **fair**."

▼ This Western Union office helped send weather reports around the country.

Today, there are three different types of winter storm warnings:
• winter storm watch
• winter storm warning
• winter weather advisory

No Warning

On Saturday, forecasters knew two storms were headed toward the East Coast. One carried warm, **moist** air from the south. The other had cold air from the north.

▼ Washington, D.C. gets hit by the Blizzard of 1888.

The southern storm was supposed to move out to sea. The northern storm was considered harmless. The southern storm went to sea, but turned around. The warm, moist air hit against the cold air and created a blizzard.

Heavy snow began falling on Sunday in Washington, D.C. Ice coated the telephone and telegraph wires. The weight made the wires snap. Contact was cut off. Washington couldn't warn New York about the blizzard.

The Blizzard of 1888 hit all the "red" states.

When warm air bumps into cold air, storms are likely. The greater the difference in temperature, the worse the storms may be.

The School Children's Blizzard

This blizzard was not the first to strike without warning that year. On January 12, a blizzard hit Nebraska and other Great Plains states as schools were letting out. The storm reached as far south as Texas. It became known as the School Children's Blizzard.

The morning had been warm and fair. By the afternoon, temperatures had fallen 60 to 70 degrees. The wind roared. **Snowdrifts** as big as barns blocked the roads. Kids crawled through cornfields and hid in haystacks. The storm killed many people, including teachers and students who froze to death.

▼ Fort Niobrara after the blizzard hit Nebraska

During this blizzard, a part of the Colorado River that runs through Texas froze. The ice was one foot thick. No one had ever seen this happen before.

Walking to Work

On March 12, 1888, Meta's school was closed because of the snow. She and other kids stayed home. The adults, however, went to work. Otherwise, they wouldn't get paid.

▼ An "el" train taking people to work in New York City in 1884

Some jobs were miles away. Workers in Brooklyn, New York, usually crossed the river by boat. Workers in New York City rode trolleys and trains on high tracks, called els. Now the river was frozen. Trolleys weren't running. The els were stuck in the snowdrifts.

Everyone had to walk, but nobody was prepared. Uncovered ears turned white from the cold. People cut holes in cardboard boxes and used them for covering.

In very cold weather it's important to wear gloves, a hat, and layers of clothing. Layers trap air, which helps keep a person warm.

A Dangerous City

The streets of New York were a death trap. The wind could knock a person into a building or under a horse's hoof. A person might fall into a 60-foot snowdrift or be hit with sharp pieces of flying coal from the open bins.

▲ New Yorkers stand behind one of the many snowdrifts after the Blizzard of 1888.

Danger was found above the streets, too. Thousands of miles of electric, telephone, and telegraph wires were strung on poles. The wind blew down the ice-coated wires. Sparking wires lay twisted in the snow like deadly snakes. People and horses became tangled in the wires and were **shocked** or killed.

Some poles were 90 feet high and carried up to 200 separate wires.

Hungry and Cold

When people got home from work, they faced more problems. Their houses were dark and cold. Their children were hungry.

▲ Families in wealthy areas had enough food to last throughout the blizzard.

Rich families, like Meta's, kept large supplies of food and coal for their stoves. Poor people bought only enough goods to last for one day. Some stores tried to make money by charging high prices. Other shops were closed or had nothing left to sell. The supply ships had sunk at sea. The **harbor** was frozen and no new goods could be brought in.

People burned their furniture to keep warm. They ate snow. Many became sick or died from hunger.

About 100 sailors lost their lives during the storm.

NEW YORK HERALD,
MARCH 13, 1888.

SNOWBOUND.

New York's Mighty Pulse Almost Stilled by a Terrible Storm.

RAGING WIND AND BLINDING DRIFT.

The City's Busiest Thoroughfares Turned Into Scenes of Winter Desolation.

TRAVEL AND BUSINESS PARALYZED.

Only One "L" Road Attempts to Run and the Horse Cars Give Up Altogether.

TELEGRAPH AND TELEPHONE WIRES DOWN.

Ferryboats Struggling with the Storm and Trains Snowed Up in the Country.

NEW YORK HERALD,
MARCH 14, 1888.

THE BURIED CITY

New York's Dreadful Sepulture Under Masses of Snow.

NIGHT OF DEVASTATION.

Tempest Howled and Raged Through the Dark Wilderness of Streets.

MEN AND WOMEN

Going Underground

On March 14, the blizzard ended. The storm killed 400 people, 200 of them in New York. It left thousands hurt and homeless. The blizzard got people thinking about ways to make the city safer.

▲ New York City officials and police officers take a look at the first subway.

Years earlier, a man named Alfred Beach wanted New York to have underground trains. At that time, people weren't so sure. Now they remembered the els stuck on the high tracks. Beach's idea made sense. Work began on the **subway** system in 1894.

Power lines strung up on poles were taken down and put underground. Today, wires are underground in many cities.

▲ A New York City subway station today

The subways help New Yorkers get around more quickly during bad weather.

Cleaning Up

Blowing coal had hurt people during the storm. Garbage in the street rotted after the snow melted. New Yorkers knew it was time to clean up their streets. The city started a group to get rid of snow and garbage. It was called the Department of Sanitation. It still does these jobs today.

People could no longer have open coal bins on the sidewalk. Boxes couldn't be piled up where they might fall on somebody. New rules made signs and fences safer. The Blizzard of 1888 helped New York become a safer place.

▲ A one-horse wagon and garbage collector clean New York City's streets in 1888.

◀ Even before the Blizzard of 1888, New York City streets were often filled with garbage.

Wind can blow harder in cities than in other places. It can get trapped between tall buildings, causing a "wind tunnel."

Weather 24-7

People understood that the country needed a better weather forecasting system. The U.S. Weather Service was formed in 1876. Soon after the Blizzard of 1888, it began to cover the weather around the country 24 hours a day, 7 days a week.

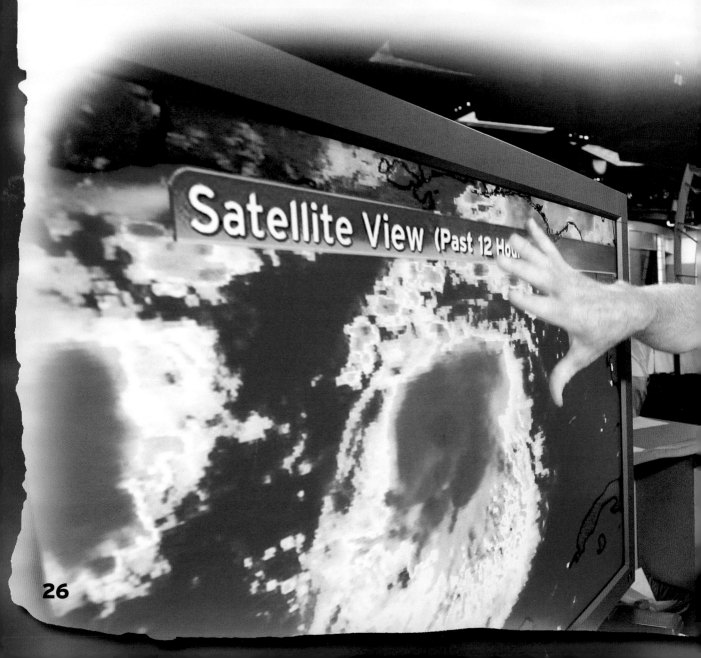

Today, scientists who study the weather use computers and **satellites** to track storms. Weather reports are on TV and the radio, day and night.

Meta was a real girl. She lived through the blizzard because her parents were prepared. Today, everyone has the information needed to be ready. We can all live through a blizzard.

◀ Dr. Steve Lyons, from The Weather Channel, tracks a storm.

Computers pull together information about weather to show if a storm is coming.

Just the Facts

Other U. S. blizzards have also made their mark on history

- **The Great Snow of 1777**—This blizzard brought high winds and three feet of snow to New England. Many animals died because it was so cold.
- **The Blizzard of 1899**—This blizzard lasted for four days in February 1899. It covered more than half of the Northeast. It's known as the Snow King.
- **Storm of the Century**—On March 13-14, 1993, this blizzard hit states from Alabama to Massachusetts. It wasn't just a blizzard. It brought tornadoes, thunderstorms, and floods, too.

There were many problems caused by the Blizzard of 1888

- 50 trains got trapped between stations.
- 15,000 people were caught in the cold.
- 200 boats were stuck at sea.
- 20-40 inches of snow hit New York and New England.
- Snowdrifts were as high as 60 feet.
- 20 million dollars in repairs were needed.

New York City and other cities in the United States are now safer because

- Telephone and electric wires are mostly underground.
- Many train tracks are underground.
- There are more garbage laws.
- There are weather forecasts 24 hours a day, 7 days a week.

There are now three different types of winter storm warnings that forecasters use

- winter storm watch—a major winter storm is likely to happen over the next 36 hours.
- winter storm warning—a major winter storm is about to start or is happening now.
- winter weather advisory—bad winter weather or a storm is likely to occur or is happening.

Glossary

blizzard (BLIZ-urd)   a storm with very strong winds, temperatures under 20°F, and hard blowing snow that lasts for at least three hours

conditions (kuhn-DISH-uhnz)   things that are needed before something else can happen

effect (uh-FEKT)   what happens because of something

fair (FAIR)   clear; not cloudy or stormy

features (FEE-churz)   important qualities or parts of something

forecasts (FOR-kasts)   statements about what you think might happen in the future

harbor (HAR-bur)   a protected part of a body of water where ships rest or unload goods

hurricane (HUR-uh-*kane*)   a storm with very high winds and heavy rain

moist (MOIST)   slightly wet

satellites (SAT-uh-lites)   spaceships or other objects sent into space that send information back to earth

shocked (SHOKD)   received a strong charge of electricity through the body

snowdrifts (SNOH-*drifts*)   piles of snow created by the wind

snowstorms (SNOH-*stormz*)   storms with winds and snow

subway (SUHB-*way*)   an electric train or system of trains that runs underground in a city

telegraph (TEL-uh-*graf*)   a way to send messages over long distances using a code of electrical signals

30

Bibliography

Library of Congress. *American Life Histories: Manuscripts from the Federal Writers' Project, 1936–1940.* (http://memory.loc.gov/ammem/wpaintro/wpahome.html)

Lilienthal, Meta. *Dear Remembered World: Childhood Memories of an Old New Yorker.* New York, NY: Richard R. Smith (1947).

Strong, Samuel Meredith. *The Great Blizzard of 1888.* New York, NY (1939).

Read More

Burby, Liza N. *Blizzards.* New York, NY: PowerKids Press/Rosen Publishing Group, Inc. (1999).

Chambers, Catherine. *Blizzard.* Chicago, IL: Heinemann Library (2002).

Murphy, Jim. *Blizzard.* New York, NY: Scholastic, Inc. (2000).

Osborne, Will and Mary Pope Osborne. *Twisters and Other Terrible Storms: A Nonfiction Companion to* <u>Twister on Tuesday</u> (Magic Tree House Research Guide). New York, NY: Random House Books for Young Readers (2003).

Learn More Online

Visit these Web sites to learn more about blizzards:

http://www.infoplease.com/spot/blizzard1.html

http://www.weather.com/encyclopedia/winter/index.html

Index

About the Author

Jacqueline A. Ball has written and produced more than one hundred books for kids and adults. She lives in New York City and Old Lyme, Connecticut.